Moments *of* **Love**

Copyright © 2013 Damarcus Wigfall P/K/A Dmarkis Wigfall

Cover & Book layout: **steve**mckinnis.com
Dmarkis photo: Chantal Pasag

All rights reserved. All rights reserved, including the right to reproduce this book or potions thereof in any form whatsoever. For information email at dmarkiswigfall@gmail.com
Printed in the United States

ISBN: **978-0-9844296-4-6**

To *my* **friends**

Who always show *me* **love**

For Hawke

Moments *of* **Love**

Dmarkis Wigfall

Contents

06 Forward
08 Questions
09 Untitled
10 February 2000
11 Believe
12 I am Mark's broken Heart
13 Exist
14 It's Gone
15 The Past
16 Questioning
18 Where did you go?
19 Who stole your heart?
20 Say Something
21 Trapped
22 September 25, 2002
23 what's in store
24 Infatuation
26 Billy
27 lust filled wall
28 muse
29 Untitled; infatuation
30 talk to me
31 greetings
32 just right
33 hide
34 ten fingers
35 moments
37 simple
33 crazy
38 fitting
39 drops
40 ice
41 kiss
42 repair what's broken
43 Ten Thousand Ways
44 Sometimes we fall
45 Time with you
46 walk away
47 passing by
48 summers dream
49 love heals
50 mixed up
51 tell the truth
52 waiting for love
53 superman
54 stranger
55 summer day
56 intoxicating

57 addicted to love
59 three doors
60 it doesn't hurt
61 empty
62 passer by
63 fleeting
64 aches for me
65 timmins
66 my first love
67 connections
68 rose colored
69 hold me
70 cliché
71 take the time
73 give it away
74 worthy
75 why
76 defining love
78 sincerely
79 good bye
80 say YES
81 Paint my life red
82 a fool for you
84 come down
85 swimming
86 waiting, part 2
87 the call
89 feels like home
89 suddenly
91 something new
92 you
93 secret place
94 falling
96 change of heart
97 beauty in ashes
98 depths below
100 picture perfect
102 I pour out
103 you were made for me
105 in my mind
106 it won't always be like this
108 two hearts
109 pitfall
110 God smiles
111 pillow talk
112 lost
113 quote
114 epilogue

5

Foreword

Love is one of the most elusive and complex of emotions. It's difficult to comprehend, let alone possess. Love can mend torn hearts, wage wars and save lives. Love can bring about peace or rebuild a nation and perhaps transform skeptics, like me, into full blown believers in this '*Crazy little thing called* ***LOVE'.***

After three decades of seeing others, including myself, "fall" in love (or reject it), my thoughts began to expound upon what love really is, and how its long term after effects can turn people's world upside down. The roller coaster of highs and lows can take a toll on one's psyche, but at the same time, it can bring us closer to the core of understanding what "love" is all about. When I was young I believed that I was incapable of love. I had no clue as to what love would be or what it would feel like. Because I spent most of my time as a child acting like a parent, I only knew discipline. As a result, I resented the adults in my life. In my alone time I felt my situation could be different, that the world was full of things that could bring me pleasure and relief from the mundane existence I was living as a child. But this thing called "love" was still a mystery.

Being the first child of seven and for many years the only child, I felt isolated from family members. As an adult this isolation would transform and resurface as independence. These factors led to a strong fear of any commitment. I would over analyze any personal relationship which played out well into my early thirties causing quite a bit of turmoil. Looking back, my formative memories are mainly about my grandmother and time spent with her and the bond we shared. My role with my Mother was as her best friend, not her child. Both of these relationships are the central part of my emotional being. It took me a great deal of time to understand my feelings of separation and neglect caused by these primary figures.

My parents were young lovers and never married so, as a result, I had two families. My mother's family was very affectionate. They expressed emotion verbally through saying "I love you" and physically through hugs and kisses. My Father's family was a stark contrast; I always felt there was a barrier of space between the words, never voiced, and the physicality of the emotion within my paternal family. Having to spend the bulk of my time with his family, the power of nonverbal communication and a passive-aggressive nature is what I absorbed and utilized. Seeing, experiencing and feeling these differences of showing affection created a deep pocket of buried emotions growing up. I had no idea these feelings would return much later in life for me to deal with again. Through counseling I learned to confront my issues and how to better express them. I was intent about diligently working through them. It took many hours in therapy practicing how to positively interact. Through falling in love and letting go of that love I've learned not to fear the negative repercussions of saying, "I love you."

Past hurts have propelled me through an evolution of connections, though some parts of my life are still tainted by those pains. I have since decided to delve into the core of the matter: relationships. My positive role models were from the female's perspective in my childhood and adolescence. Due to the lack of consistency, that "blue print" did not serve me well. I needed some concrete coupling in order to see the interaction of people being in partnerships and the progress from that effort. Since there were no immediate ones to observe, the lessons came after I left home and began maturing and socializing with people outside of my family.

The awakening for love started in Sherman, a small Texas town at the age of thirteen with my first crush. It was just a taste, but with each new person I trusted in, flourished a new emotion. All seemingly fresh and foreign, I began to allow myself to take chances and explore what was possible and available to me as I graduated from school and left for the navy traveling from coast to coast. I have learned about infatuation, lust, lying, guilt, loss and how it feels to be truly heartbroken. I have understood how to compromise and when not to, how to hope, how to follow my intuition and how, despite all else, love. It was almost burdensome to really uncover myself, but the joy and freedom of letting go set me free to love.

I am a student of love. Through these tests, failures and successes I continued to understand that I wanted to know more; to be engulfed by **LOVE** in order to give it back. The following writings are portions of my life, my loves in prose and in rhyme. Some are life lessons and others about people who've left an indelible mark on my life and my heart. Some are about what could have been.

"Life is given in a child
realized in the old person and cherished as an adolescent.
The stages of our purpose are to interact, learn, respond and grow.
Those who don't follow will be left behind, wasted or even frowned upon.
Their life, hanging in the distance
no guidance, no maturity, no completion.
Who wants to simply exist?
That is what happens with no purpose.
You/I become fillers for the universe.
The world we live in continues not to look at us as contributors,
but as a bug who serves no one, no good, no purpose."

-Dmarkis Wigfall

Questions

I have often wondered why I was placed on this earth. Usually these thoughts occupy my mind while in a very low place and feeling pretty badly about myself. It just happens to work out that way and although I don't plan it out, it does bring up the question of self worth and why, *"Oh god why?"* in a dramatic fashion.

People, I believe, do take their lives because they can't deal with these unanswered questions. We are susceptible to allowing outside influences to override the love we should have inside.

Questioning life has often gotten me into a world of trouble and low self esteem.

My negative thoughts overwhelmed me to the point that I was hospitalized and medicated in order to stabilize my mind. I was torn because my heart said one thing, but society and religion said I should be another. I could no longer live under the expectation of everyone else so I had to ask myself; who am I living for?

Untitled

How long must we go on through life pretending and hiding?

The hurt on the inside and the mask on the outside?

How can we smile when our hearts and minds are endlessly wandering?

The peace we long for is far away and the joy is gone

Sadness has encompassed us and has held our spirits hostage

What must we do to wake up and experience a newness of life?

When will this suffering end?

Who will save us from the destruction that is before us?

As beauty appeals to us

It is all we see and the least of our needs

When the lights of our world go out

Then we will see each other as we should, not with out eyes but with our hearts

My belief system has shaped most of my opinions that I hold dear, and on the other hand has also been a limiting factor for growth in my personal life because I allowed it to push out things that were necessary in accepting myself and others. Balance is the key, and yes I still do pray.

February 5, 2000

> *"Well God you know my heart*
> *And the things I don't speak that eat away at my soul*
> *The things I dare not to speak to anyone about*
> *For fear of what will become of me.*
>
> *My life would surely be different*
> *If I could only be honest with myself and the part I hate."*

Believe

Never stop believing,
Never falter on the ideas that you hold dear

Always trust in these things that are part of you.
For in them is the reality of life,
your life

Failing to believe means not accepting in you.
That you are limitless,
and it is so untrue to conceive that.

Belief will out live all theory, fiction, and indecisiveness
that may be imparted in your inner man.

Because we believe, we are
and because we are
we believe.

Don't ever give up believing!

I am Mark's broken Heart

To find truth when there are all lies

To find peace when the gale seems to have overtaken me

To drink when I am thirsty

To squelch the desire of loneliness

To smile when the sun has risen

Casting a shadow on my problems

To breathe when I am suffocated by hatred

To awaken when I realize it was all a mirage

And the refreshing water that was once there is gone, all gone

An image of what is supposed to have been

Exist

What good is life without love?

What good is love without life?

Both of these need each other

And depend on the other

Without one both would cease to exist.

It's Gone

Love lost, love found
Love here, love now
It's just not the same without you here with me

A smile, a touch
Something I wanted so much
But love's gone and I'm here by myself

Love's here, love's now
Sometimes I wonder how
When what I feel is low
And the memory won't leave me alone

So why can't I change
When these feelings get in the way?

Love's here for now then it's gone.

Love should've shielded me from a broken heart
Instead it led me in without a guard.

The Past

How to let you go after I loved you for so long
You comforted me when loneliness suffocated my sunshine
And darkness slept with me

Your love was deep, moving, enticing,
But all the while destroying the very life in me
What to do without you?

My friend, my foe; the love-hate relationship we share
You could be warm
Then cold
Abrupt yet gentle
How I long to savor it all.

Without you, that even sounds strange
I would feel like a child in the woods
All by myself
Starting over from step one,
without you,

Learning to walk without you
Being happy without you
You whom I have loved
for a lifetime

Questioning

We spend all our time together

Going wherever

In the rain, in the snow, hiking, bike riding, or just eating tacos.

We laugh at the same corny jokes

Like the same tunes, sleep in each others beds, stay up to watch the moon.

At lunch we meet for a quick bite,

Talk about the weather and what's on our minds

How your boss sucks and how I love mine

We chat about when we are going to the gym

How much time we get to spend in it,

We talk about the weekend and the movies we should see

How you have been talking to this girl

Which no one ever gets to meet?

And how you can never find anyone who supplies your needs,

Then we make plans to visit each others parents

Take a trip up the coast, we smile, sing and laugh

and

take photos

and bake.

Two hours, three weeks, four months and a day
We can't get enough of each other,
But still you can't stay

You spend most of your time with me,

But still you won't allow us to be,

I like you and you like me

If you haven't found her by now

Then it occurs to me,

That you don't know yourself and you really don't know me.

people such as us

As close as we are,

It should be clear that we are something more than just friends

Questioning who you are was never an issue to me

But you have to be honest with yourself so you can be free.

Question the air that blows

Question the stock markets which are bound to go down

Question the trends, the analyst, and the leaves

Question the psychics that seem to know the way

Have doubt in everything that you believe,

But never question that there is more to you than the eye can see.

Where did you go?

Where did you go?
I am still here waiting for you to come again
I imagined you would
take away my sorrow
sleep with me, hold me
Make me smile

How have you been?
I have been okay without you
No more hurt
No more wondering
No more unanswered questions.

I left you so long ago
I forgot what you felt like.

Who stole your heart?

Who stole your heart?
Where did it go?

Once so cold
But now it shows

Someone got to you
Because you have changed

The once distant playboy
Has now become a man

Just like the rest of us who grieve and feel pain
You now have emotion to match a name

Who stole your heart?
Who got to you?

I am glad it happened because I feel it too

Say Something

Say Something to me
It doesn't matter what it would be
All the words in the world
Yet you want to remain silent.

You stand there and watch
But will you ever speak
I think not
Why I don't know.

Why do you stare?
What the hell's going on in there?
Your mind that is
Would something please give?

I've spoken
I've tried
But the situation juxtaposed
Still relies
On you to say something so I can know
Whether or not to move on

Trapped

Trapped inside, what to decide
I just want to escape this place

I struggle, I drown
No hope be found
I wonder aimlessly

Keep it all together, be strong be together
No hurt, no pain to show or remain

All lies, all deceit
This pain is killing me

I can't go on, I was never that strong
When was my change to come?

The days go by, why is it I have to lie
Where is my relief?

These ups, these downs
Oh my God what now?
Who will save me from myself?
I pray, I try
I fail, I fly
High above to escape myself
forever trapped

waiting

"Trying to get myself together for a life changing move I can feel fear and anxiety building in my mind making me want to do the unthinkable"

What to do. Where to go.
Who can help, who can know
Suffering inside making poetry and song
It seems unreal to continue on
Change has come, its at my door
With it love and hope to usher me on
Contentment right behind
With prosperity next in line
Waiting…waiting for me to let them in

what's in store

Trying to find what love is, what is life?
Is it just a passing feeling?

With time we find the truth inside
searching and longing for this moment

reality seems to be fading and fleeting
leaving us with no hope for tomorrow

too late in life we make mistakes
Failing and falling
continually trying to see if this is all there is

to live for love
and when will it show

day after day the same trials take place
in everyone looking to overcome?

soon, in time, we will find that thing
that we have all waited for
it will be so much more

because there has to be something more to life
past the pain,
the grief,
and the strife

moving on into a new world
I'll just hang on longer for what's in store

Infatuation

"Before I met you I had already loved you. We had not spoken or seen each other; but by what strength were we bound to be? The flesh indeed craves after your touch, to feel your warm body, to make passionate love.

Now that you are here I have understood the part that longed for you has evolved into something much more. The innocence that I once embraced found in you without a trace of unnatural desire only sheer respect.

Divided between love that will never cease and one that shouldn't be loses me in a mist that's drawn from the sea. Foul thoughts cannot dare enter into our arena. Foggy, now clouded intuition. On track and focused. Dreading to love and fail, I attempt to find out.

It was not I but you who called. Wide eyed and interested standing there tall. Nothing to offer. What was the price we were to pay?"

what's if?

Have you ever had a feeling that you just had to know someone or be around them no matter what? For some reason they just draw you into their world just by being or maybe the scenario is you really respect a person's character, or like the way they dress, or the way they handle people or make you feel by just watching them?

There is this strange chemistry that happens to you with some random stranger or even a person you have known for a while but can't explain it? This happens to me often!

I have had numerous conversations with people about love and usually I have a question that I ask them when I find out if they are married or in long-term relationships and it's usually; *"How did you know?"*

I say it starts with infatuation. It's that little nudging interest of *"What if?"* or maybe, *"I like you"*.

To me the definition of infatuation is a genuine unwarranted interest in someone or something. Usually this is how much of my writing gets started because a spark of interest moves my imagination to *"What if?"*

These feelings of interest can open my mind to possibilities I've never dreamt and also propel me into relationships either real or fictional that create art, love, and memories which can last a lifetime.

Billy

I met you and was immediately afraid
Your charm and simple ways
Thrown off guard by what I thought would never be,
We spoke and exchanged "hello" graciously

Never knowing what was to come or that you would be a participant in the front row
In the audience of players talented and free
Dancing and prancing for all to see

In a moment there you were again
But in different light and as a friend

We parted not to assume
All was over next Friday
Many hours past noon

One, two, three, four how much alcohol is needed? More?
One meeting just to acquaint, the second to admire again,
The third to enter into a torrid romance

We talked, we laughed, we danced
And held each other through the night
Forgetting time and who was around

What arose from the settled dust was no longer just me
But an us

lust filled wall

Phone calls, conversations, freedom and now relations
Two worlds entering
one at the beginning and one at the end

Five, six, seven dates later and how do we really feel?
Do we still caress?
Do we still adore?
Or has this relationship become another bore?

It is hard to tell what is real and what is not
When your emotions have been mangled in serious knots

Twisted and turned, balled up and dropped
Made into different colors and fragmented materials

Some to wear, some to share, some to give away, some to pack for
a rainy day
But what is real, where is the love?
Who has it? And is there enough?

How can someone with so little experience at all
Decipher the language of love written on a lust filled wall

My muse

"You are my muse. You're a constant reminder of how simple and beautiful life can be. You consume me, the thought of you makes me weak and fearful; not of danger, but for the complete adoration I feel for you.

I see your name and images of your smile overshadow my thoughts. Your face I see clearly as though you were standing next to me. I remember your touch, your voice, all time stops when your skin brushes mine.

How we could cause the earth to shudder at our union as if two distant stars colliding into each other forming galaxies and planets.

How I need you, you that pulls at the heart of me, even the soul of my desire! Will you appease me? Won't you hear me? Will you ever take a chance on me as I would with you?

The miles have separated us the years have pushed us, but fate will bring us together once again. I will have you. It will be you. I love you.

You rescued my fleeting heart from despair. You saw beauty where only disappointment had lain. You looked past the skin, the flaws, and the masks to see me."

UNTITLED (infatuation)

tingles in my hand anxious to touch yours
minutes turn into wasted hours
just to be close to you

I can't stop these feelings from multiplying
being near you

I didn't know this feeling would be there for you
but here it is stronger by the day
tougher by the minute I am apart from you

I wonder what it is that you do to make me feel this way that I do
but I cannot deny my unbridled passion to be with you

Drawn to you
I deny myself
I wait, loving another
hoping one day you would no longer be afraid to be yourself
around me

the closer I get the more I feel
the further away the less I need

the absence kills me inside
just to be close then closer
to hold, to help, to keep
you

Talk to Me

Let me hear the words you no longer speak
that used to fall from your lips
so bittersweet
Once more my ear is attentive
to hear those words. If you talk to me.
Silence can be such an unforgiving thing
used like a weapon in the games we play
still I long to read your lips, to
touch your words with my fingertips
put them closely to mine and listen to you.
talk to me.
Regretting sometimes these lyrics that I write
but hoping you read them so you know that I am alive
hoping you can read between the lines
it's about you
hoping you can read between the line
and me
but this is just an illusion, my pipe dream,
yearning for you to talk to me.

greetings

Travel with me my sweet one
to the furthest parts of my mind
into the depths of my soul
open the eyes of my heart so that I may see you clearly
in days passing
in eve while dreaming
come stay with me here
within me so that you may know me.
in love

just right

i needed water
and you let me drink,
i was hungry,
you fed me
i was lonely,
you held me
i was sad,
you comforted me
i was lost,
you found me.

hide beneath the shadow

the torment grew daily as i sat
counting the minutes, punishing my eyelids
to keep awake.

the doors closed, the windows wide open
the sun my sole companion grazes across the sky above.

i counted the stars til they were turned to day,
i watched the moon until it disappeared too.

i searched my soul for you,
relief,
release,
moments

so that i could be free of you o'
broken heart of mine.

air would not enter my lungs for it
was choked out between my lips which would not part
for fear of speaking your name.

escape i could not,
though try i did
to leave this sordid memory and hide

but where i turned there you were my shadow.

Joy to the World

ten fingers and ten toes
dark brown eyes and a cute round nose

precious sounds made by you when laying in my arms.

the smell of your new baby skin permeates the room,
as does your smile, your warmth.

the joy that leaped out of my chest and into my life
made me wonder, made me cry

never thinking you could be a reality
but here you are small and sweet.

untarnished, untouched, and not vexed by the world,
your smiles are pure,
your laughter is real
you are a joy to the world.

moments

in the rain
in the green grass and trees
in flowers blooming in spring
in a look
into the windows of our soul
in a freckle
in a mole
in a shapely figure
in thinning hair
in a smile
in a cry
in humility, in a stare
in triumph
in our loss
in death, in life, in us all
there is beauty in these moments.

It's simple

i dreamed of a love,
one that would consume me
lift me up past the celestial bodies
that dangle in the abyss

that love which engulfs my being

lost

in time and space.

in fleeting moments
it abides, not life, nor death
would desecrate this beauty that remains

from that feeling of eternal bliss
when you are in love.

I'm Crazy About You

I couldn't get close enough to you
if I were your skin it still wouldn't be enough

I sit at your door thinking of ways to make you smile
because you are my sunshine

I dream of ways to keep you satisfied
so your heart will know it has a home

Were you walk I want to be your shadow

Can I be your lips too?
so that I can feel your breath on me all day?

I want to be close to you

fitting in

a part of my life gone missing
but looking back where would I have "*fit in*"

told to live in a life not my own,
but deciding to find that life on another road.

questioning what to do and if it was me
or just a joke, some calamity

that would make this internal struggle so hard
to balance love, desire, passion, and God.

i watched, i waited, i lied, then i lived
finding out later it was my choice to give

to be happy with me completely
and there i was truly free
appreciating what was inside me
i finally fell in love with me

drops on petals

raindrops painting our skin in a soft mist
caressing our petals of flesh as morning dew shimmers
soft, subtle, and sweet
seamless we were under the lights
blending arms and legs and torsos together
there in your arms
i felt safe, i felt one with you
no space between us
not even the air could separate the
ember that burned within

Black diamond's on White Ice

swirls of ice falling like angels to the ground

the air cold, brisk, chilling to the bone

the flickering of black diamonds in the sky

made the night even more magical.

Slow moving cars in the distance almost too far to recognize

and the aroma of wood burning scented on the wind

a setting for romance.

Holding hands, innocence is stolen

entwined in sweetness and honesty

beguiled of a kiss

frozen forever in time.

the kiss

the taste of your lips on mine
craving you more and more

the pulse of your blood
under my fingertips heating my desire,
calling me into your arms
feeding the intensity in my soul

insecurity escapes me with every gentle kiss
there under your chest, with every exhale

i feel you closer, closer than ever
and i am safe, i am loved.

Repair What's Broken

I mended my heart
after you stole it away
as a raven plucking pieces on the ground
after it had been broken.

scattered it was
over the streets
littered amongst strangers

surely it was meant to be put together again
by skillful hands in an artful form

structured and strengthened
with ties of patience

bonding what was damaged
tempering that which was weak

fortifying that which was once
delicate with trust, passion, and above all else; love

ten thousand ways

ten thousand ways to make love to you
played out in my sleep.

how to hold you
caress you
kiss you
and take you.

thinking about the ways to please you
to engulf you
to ravish you
to entice you
to get you into my arms.

to laugh with you
to cuddle with you
to smile at you
to be with you.

sometimes we fall

who said, " love will save the day?"
I say sometimes it can get in the way
once normal people sane and determined
fall foot over head into this emotion of love
leaving all clarity and sound reasoning behind
just for that feeling of falling for someone.
We close our eyes and jump off the bridge
not knowing if water or concrete will be at the bottom.
excited for that first step
getting high on the way down
hurt by the impact
and then chronicling it the next few days.
we go blindly for some
and others we know upfront
the details that will either make or break what time we share.
but still we go and jump just to fall into this thing called love.

spend more time with you

spending time with you
walks through the park
talking much about nothing
wasting time just being with you
the ease at which we are
just you and i side by side
makes me smile
and then i sigh
thankful to be spending time with you
the closer you are the more i enjoy
the brush of your arm
the pitch in your voice
it feels good to be spending time with you
the sun lights the day
I am anxious to see your face
begging the night not to come
so I can spend more time with you

just walk away

time waited for us just this night
we held each other close, so tight

i knew you would be leaving
you knew i wanted you to stay

but i had to let you
just walk away

I question whether you were here unintentionally
or was it just a fog of deceit

that i could have you
and let you walk away

Passing by

the bed so cold without you in it
but your scent remains on the pillows from the night before

i rest my head on my arm just to get another drink of your scent you left on mine
I folded the sheets atop my body to collect warmth were you once lay

but grasp you i could not
you were already gone.

i ponder your time here with me
i pray that you would greet me with the sun

i stroked your hair as you slept
i smelled your breath as you exhaled onto my neck

morning came all to quick
and so ended our romance

you were only passing by.

a mid-summer's dream

If someone could tell our story what would they say?

we are two lovers living two lives and too far away.

I play your emotions, and you step on mine

I find your weakness, you take your time

deliberately with your facade

painstakingly holding on to a lie

burdening my heart that I want to deliver to you

but how?

I give you this chance and you reject me as often you do,

but love you I do, and this i will always know is true.

One day you will awake, and see

my love, my strength, which you have gained.

One day you will see that you are my mid-summers dream.

love heals

a sad murmur in my stomach
i look up at the grey skies,
the water falling from the blanket of clouds just over head and out
of reach

i begin to think of the lives intertwined with mine
i think about the ones that have changed me
I remember the ones i have affected

i am grateful.

i think of the hands that held mine when i was hurt
the ones that touched my cheek so softly when I was sad
the hands that patted me on the back when i was proud

those are the ones i cling to, and hold on to for dear life when
everything else seems as dark as these clouds above my head
and I see because of love
i am healed.

mixed up

sullen
soundless
simple
subdued
secretive
sorrowful

perplexed at emotions that seem to have not arisen from a safe place

afraid of words that would destroy

conflicted by morals but propelled by truth

desire forgotten in romantic illusion

is the world a dream?

locked

longing

lust

loss

components often together further complicating the mind

away they are, further pushed away they shall be.

until reality sets in and I reveal the real me.

tell the truth

praying for answers and reasons

watching time drift
another wrinkle, another pain inside
the knees give out, the back is sore, you're tired

the one thing that matters is what i look for
the connection of lives

the thread that pulls us all together
and in the direction we are headed.

the mystery of the unknown is a perplexing thing
to live life to your best ability and yet have it be a question burning
in your head

this life that we only get one of,
why does it all matter, to whom does it matter, and when will it
matter.

this life.

waiting for love

Whatever happened to true love
is it really an imaginary thing that is unattainable?

where does the desire and passion that follows
the initial meeting and greeting go?

is it now that we settle for less
that we give up the best

The best of ourselves and that hope of
being completely, truly, and deeply in love.

What happened to the love
the one that makes us move across the country
denying everyone else for one more embrace from the object of our desire

that "25 years later" and still smiling love
wake-up wanting to hold you love
take me anywhere love
kiss me everywhere kind of love
I can't get enough of you love.

Superman

My day starts with you, seeing that sharp smile looking at those bright blue eyes

That strut in your stride, I grin as you walk by. Damn i think you are fine.

Your voice rich as molasses as you search my face, filling the air with silly unnecessary chatter, I embrace the words just to pass the time and savor each syllable.

But fine doesn't hit the mark, incredible is more like it, breathtaking would be an understatement.

If I was looking for superman, i would picture you as a hero, standing tall, helping the weak, saving the poor.

rescuing my heart.

Stranger

two more kisses then you have to go
I only planned on seeing you once then nothing more.

playing roulette with the pictures in my hand
whose eyes find mine, who is a real man.

looking to see you, are you the real deal,
can I laugh with you, how do I really feel.

I push my fears to the background of my mind
in order to focus on your hands
not my hearts pounding sound.

I had only gained enough courage to say hello
but here I am now laying in your bed

better than the picture
glad that I am with you
but you are just a stranger to me

I had only planned to say hello.

just a summer day

the sun drenched the bamboo deck with an ethereal glow
dripping warmth over our bodies
the breeze from the west cooled the sweat that formed on his shoulders.
the wood pressed hard against my back as his lean hard body caressed my skin
and his lips travelled the length of my neck.
my focus: his thighs on mine, the sound of the stream behind, the rustle of the wind through the trees, and the pants of slow breathing as we made love.
with every thrust of his waist my body shuddered with passion, wanting and longing for more
my eyes fluttered to focus on his
my heart racing to match the thunderous beat of his
my trembling arms failed to hold him any closer
as we collapse into the warmth of the day
in love
in harmony
in each other.

Intoxicating

I watch the air rise under the sheets
lifting your chest slow, rhythmically

the exhale of your breath
tickles my nose

and I brush your brow ever so softly with my finger as you sleep

your eyelids flutter and i know you are resting peacefully and soundly

I touch your hair

and you are still

I touch your soft pink lips moistened by mine

you pull me closer and I drift with you into slumber

warmth radiating from you heats my chilly legs and cheeks

and I nestle closer to you

capturing your sweet scent,

the aroma of love.

the sun parts the trees, glowing on the white sheets and pillow cases

you smile as you say goodbye.

I blink just to get a glimmer of you walking away

and cuddle the bed which is saturated with the smell of you

my arm, my sheets, my fingers, my pillow

I stay in bed longer just to have you near me still.

addicted to love

i spent hours and days thinking about you and dreaming of you

writing sonnets and words

paragraphs and lines

mesmerized by your beauty

which comes in many forms

your lashes, your smile, your bright eyes, your legs and your thighs

the way you walk the way you talk

even the pitch in your voice can set me off.

your confidence, the way you hold your hands, the color of your hair, the way you joke with your friends

the way you look in jeans, the way you work out at the gym,

the intensity in your run, the way you eat your meals,

the full lips on your face, your thick eyebrows or your waist, the hair on your chest, the mole on your back

how you hold my hand, how you touch my skin, how you pray at night,

how you act like a man

how you cry, how you make me mad, how you remember everything, how you make plans,

how your shirt fits so nice, how you look in a suit, how you penetrate my heart

without even knowing you do

i watch you, i see, when your walls come down you are free, i like that

i guess I am just addicted to love.

three doors/two days

I knew you were trouble when I saw you
moving with a quick paced shuffle out the door and across my path.

Wondering what was about to happen, "who is this" that has moved into your space.

Rambling with words, unsettled, and impatient

anxiety laden explanations somehow you found your way in.

Weak from your approach, I let you talk on

maybe from boredom or maybe because I was alone.

The highs, the lows, inconsistency it grows

and exhausted I am with all the plans.

In a moment of truth I connected to you and reality began to set in;

that compassion it grows but addiction slows

progress and a genuine life.

I cannot be tangled with pain, the forgetfulness, nor the stains of another life that I had once known.

Let go of the things that soil your mind and let me in

to your heart

your soul

and be my friend, my lover, my everything.

It Doesn't Hurt

I patted in circles the shadows under my eyes

covering your affection with a soft beige mask.

The image reflected back at me was that of a failed and lonely heart

I smiled to think you cared for me enough to let me know when i was wrong.

My ribs still hurt from laughing so hard on our last night out,

or was it from the excitement you felt after four drinks and throwing me into the bar that day.

I've never met anyone like you who would do so many things for me

give me attention,

call me at night,

and get along with my friends,

and take me out.

With a love like yours I am complete

with all that I need except integrity or self esteem

true love doesn't hurt the outside neither is it hard

it fulfills the deepest needs and saturates my entire being

illuminating the best in all of us

complementing our spirits and beautifying everything around us

true love doesn't hurt, therefore I must let you go

no more pretending

no more scars

no more show.

Empty

the hours on the clock roll by
and the sun crosses the sky
the warmth of the day has relinquished its stand for the chill of the night

the business of the day settled into
a low murmur of routine
dinner, television, shower, sleep

i wake the next morning
the pillow is silent beside me

i stroke the place in the bed where you should be

no hands to reach back
there is no smell to reminisce.

I walk slowly through the house
wishing to hear a voice

with "good morning dear"
or "can I fix you some coffee and toast?"

but the walls are quiet
and the day has started anew

some things are the same

such as me
alone
empty, without you.

passer by

the nature of avoiding one another astounds me
the way we shift and move to ignore our simple existence
manifesting our fears and insecurities we shuffle through life in a hurried pace
ignoring the one thing that we are here for; acknowledgement and acceptance of one another

but how do we do that if not only we ignore, but brush aside our humanity and our human bonds
continually selfishly attaining more, aimlessly dredging on in the rat race of life.

forever we stare down the tunnel of our existence to the grave. We are aging but are we learning.
are we taking in the things we should know to help elevate our minds and beings to become enlightened?

i fear that we are trapped in a childlike state without persevering to the next level of consciousness repeating archaic ways of behavior and not passing down our full potential

because we are weak, we have become numb, we have been sterilized into a way of being that has not only ceased our intelligent increase but our evolutionary dominance.

we are children, all drowning at the hands of an archaic way of life with little hope of a renaissance.

people watching people starve from lack of love, higher understanding, knowledge, and wisdom

untitled

fleeting feelings fluttering in the wind
fighting age, fighting time, fighting fear

coming and going and going again
down the same road, down the same road again

faces so many laughing ones, sad ones
hopeful ones, mad ones, peaceful ones, thinking ones

which one?

tired, tossed, taken, tempted,
tempted over and over again
yielding but never wielding the power from within

to say no, not now, not ever, not with me
you are not the one, not enough, not even a piece of what i need

still yes, still giving in to the thrill of the victory
the orgasmic finish line, that will eventually set me free

tired, forgotten, forgiven, forbidden
day in and day out
sunrise, sunset the images flow freely to find another
need unmet

aches for me

who aches for me
my skin shudders
prickly, cold, aching to be held

a slow moan from within catching waves of
anguish,

long fluid movements
wrenching inward with
cravings of devotion
but lacking your presence

I am muddled and despondent
Disorientated by your vibrational pull.

the brevity of our tryst mistaken
loss forbearing over the imagination
escaping the fullest part of my intention to entice you

grasping for intimate encounters
memories breached at the moment of clarity

that in solitude
pangs of my reality
deafen the conscious mind

illusion of desire
sets a heart ablaze but with
no distinguishable recourse

not hope, not time,
no hand, no rhyme

apparitions of moments
yearned for yet no longer exist

timmins

words escape me so i created one for you
a secret word that captures the essence of your smile
and the aroma of our mingled attraction

golden, that's how i feel
dumbfounded at the mysterious intrigue
that befalls me

i watched you
eyes open, not able to turn my gaze
curious as to who you were

i watched you
as you were, knowing there was more within
but not certain

until you showed me,
golden, a heart that sings
ignites, heals, compels

shone through past the bravado
the unpolished gem, priceless and raw
deep in the earth's surface you hid

but i was the lucky one
to find, to catch a glimpse of the beauty few have seen.

first love

my first love
my only love
you left me with this hole in my heart
one with vivid memories of summer breezes thru the trees
and walks along the stony road
swimming in the river and making love on the deck.

its seems so distant now but I go there every once and awhile to remember how it felt
or rather how i felt to fall in love with you my summer love.

we spent hours laying in each other's arms
watching the sunrise until it set
the clouds would roll in bringing the cool rain and moisten the night
with its freshness.

scents of grass and trees, of wet wood and the ocean,
of newness the rain it sprinkles down.

the clouds rumble and the lightning flashes across the sky put on a show just for us as we
snuggle closer drenched in the dampness of the night storm.

my summer love how i remember
and cannot part from your picture.

lovemaking, soul tasting, learning, and growing in you.

connections

speaking words is easy
hearing them without sound,
no utterance of vowels or consonants

diction isn't needed in our conversation,
not a letter nor punctuation

we have a connection

I don't hurry to find out things about you
its like taking a slow walk through a meadow
letting the beauty unfold in every step
taking in your movements, your character
you mannerism, your faults

listening with eager ears for the questions you ask.

we have a connection that can't be explained
but drawn to you I am
comforted by you I am
intrigued by you I am.

your curiosity with me makes me blush
but as much as you query me
I also am pondering about you.

I dare not intrude in and upon your heart
for it is there I want to reside
the things i don't know may hold our innocence
and keep the mystery of this connection for another day.

rose colored

I thought you were perfection
spotless and beautiful
artistic and wild

handsome, courageous, smart, and refined
misunderstood, arrogant to a fault
your male bravado turned me on

deep and sensitive, pensive to say the least
honest with an open heart
that yearned for me

inquisitive yet reserved
stylish but not overdone,
simple in your charm
gentle and warm

I thought you were someone
whom i could share something with
my ideas, my love, my life to live

I thought many things
even when we were apart
just because I felt them and this was at the start

of knowing you then
and knowing you now

things aren't the same because
clearly I can see how

that infatuation paints a perfect picture
love covers many faults
truth and time reveals all
and things aren't so rose colored after-all

hold me

quietly suspended in fantasies
distancing reality I ask you to hold me
take me in those strong manly arms

letting the warmth penetrate the skin
deeply seeping into each layer of my flesh

tighter I say
hold me closer and tighter

energy transferring one level to the next
explanation unheard

how we become one
when you hold me

fear comes, grasp my hand
sadness around, touch my hand
hold me.

tighter i say until
i can longer feel the outside world
i no longer hear their hurtful words

i no longer am alone
when you hold me

cliché

on days such as this
trite expressions falter in subduing the emotional undercurrent

"everything happens for a reason" oh does it?

"it will all work out" will it?

"just hang in there" can I?

piecing together ideas juxtaposed in the mind
debating the cycles of human nature

torn in indecision
to go or not
to do or won't

to forgive, to release, to live

but how can we live
when noises from above and below
haunt us, making us leery of progress and redemption
taunting us with failure

mocking us with flashy unnecessary goods and gadgets
with eloquent words and fancy delicacies

"your time will come" shall it?
"the right one is out there" is he?

it's all cliché

take the time

his eyes went dim
with a six piece string in his hand
dangling from a shoddy piece of wood

the curtains were drawn
the lights were down
there was nothing left but him in his silence

he was a beauty
incomparable to most
smooth, dark features, full lips, light skin

but demons from his past
came and took his hand
and his young life was cut short

I had seen him once or twice
pondered whether to say hi
alas I chose to keep moving on

but knowing now what came about
I debate was it worth it, to not make my presence known

maybe I could have helped
or the conversation we could have had help propel
him into a different state of mind

that brought him hope and joy
just thinking of the boy
that took the time to say hello.

Often I think of things that could possibly change our lives
just moments like this that pass us by

to tell someone i love you,

to greet a stranger, to show affection, to walk up to that person you've admired or crushed on

to just take the time
that's all we have is time;

for when it has gone there is no more
death waits for no one

your impression is made daily in how you treat people, how you receive them, and how you love them

take the time
you could change a life, and in turn have yours enriched

give it away

deserving of my love
aching to be resurrected in wholeness of heart
I stand before you

broken, but not destroyed
watching the pieces swim beneath my feet
every detail of my fragmented life

from a lonely wanderer
a guarded soldier, a lover
a brother, a son, a father

told that I could never be
wishing I was all I needed
but I am desirous of your affection

wanting to let you in completely and fully
but this heart of mine is more delicate
more fragile than you know
maybe more than you can hold

more complicated than you and I

but to you I want to give it
away
this nimble heart
so that every beat remembers your name
erased is every trace of what remained

a new song to sing

that you are the one I want to send it to.

Worthy

I am worthy of your love
I am worthy of love

patience is tried
at the sight of what could be

questions of, " if only" when
you see that I am worthy

of your time
of your smile

of a moment
which is emblazoned in my psyche
taunting me daily

to which I respond, I am worthy.

often I wonder how such a one as you
could not see all that is inside of me

or why my smile is ignored
although my soul is exposed

and smitten by
the very sight of you.

I am worthy of love,
your love, hungry for it

push from me these thoughts that I
should not seek after you

but let the will take its course and
give to myself all that I need
and all that I can receive

from within.

why won't you let me?

time suspended
seated in the night
melodies drifting in the air

withdrawn from the world
we escape to our place

there we are, untouched
untainted, untroubled

you touch me
why won't you stay?

I plead with myself to let you be
but every delicious moment of your presence
compels me to want you more

more, more of you

the depth of your soul I would search
swim in the midst of your song
that sings of a love divine

In awe of you I am
wondering when and how this could ever be

hoping that at one instant you will let me

why won't you let me

in?

mistakes will be made
for sure this is not a charade

fleeting feelings depart,
because you are
the lyric to my poem
the light that shines so brightly
in the song my heart sings.

Defining Love

visiting moments of love past I ponder

was this real? or what is it this love thing that we feel?

my waking time spent dissecting the very thing
I hold dear to me; connection, emotion, not to mention, fear.

Reaching and grabbing at life's cords,
did we miss it? is there a reward?

is it a touch
is it a look

is it in words
is it in acts

is it in sorrow
is it in forgiveness

is it in compassion
is it in loss

is it defined in a quarrel
is it the amount of work or praise

is it in time
is it in money

is it in family, religion, or peace

is it feeding the hungry
or the homeless in need

or waving to a neighbor
or helping the elderly to cross the street

is it passion for what you do
or at the birth of a child
his smile so bright it lights the room?

is it in patience
is it kindness

is it tangible for us to share

this thing we know as love

what
how
who
where

sincerely

sincerely I love you
though those words were seldom said

it was shown in my smile
my gaze from across the room
in the way I stroked your hair

when I whisper softly to you
as you slumber peacefully
I gently kiss your forehead, I love you

as I hold your hand
when I rest my head upon your shoulder,
I love you

listening to your heartbeat
I wait for it to sound my name,
watching you shower in the morning
walking with you in the rain,

hearing you sing a familiar melody or getting ice cream at three...
tickling you because you hate it,
counting your toes while sitting under trees,

wanting to be near you
when we are apart,
missing your warmth
your ways
your charm

though hardly spoken those words were,
I love you, sincerely yours

goodbye

seems like I've been seeing you
seems like I have been missing you
walking down the street cars passing by
exhaust in my nose
light reflecting off quick passing windows

i count the days
the number of "I'm sorries"
"i love you's"
"forgive me's"
and all the things that we've said and done
every picture of us together
every stretch of land we treaded
and bedded

i remember the tears that i wept at losing you
and the ones shed when I found you again
i think of the lovemaking
the lip tasting
the rolling waists
and
i turn the corner
headed for the coffee calling my name
and the early morning day break

wishful thinking past
that what is left is what will last

the good

the memories of content faces

warm hand holding

mornings in bed

soft sweet memories of you and me.

i take those
store them away
pack them in my secret place
so that i can say goodbye.

Say Yes

If you'd ask me, I'd still say yes
Yes to a new me
A new you
A new us

Yes to another adventure
Another place
One more time
Yes to another chapter down the line

If you'd only ask
My heart I'd give again
Take the journey a third, fourth,
And a fifth time for sure
I would do it again

If you ask I will still say yes
For better or for worse
For more of us
Not less

Paint my life red

Tears wet the pillow as I pulled you closer
I let everything I could not say
Wash over my body as I took deep breaths of your skin
Into myself

My fingers found your hand, then your chest
I held you close hoping and praying
That you would not see my pain

But contain myself I could not as I trembled
At your side

I did not believe we were here again
The loss palpable, emanating from my pores

I stroke your brows
And my lips find yours
I definitely needed to kiss you more

Soft, warm, gentle kisses caressing my lips would be no more
I say you changed my life and
Made me a better man

Although one that could not be all you needed
But I pray that my love will remain

As those tear stained pillows remember
So shall I
Love never dies and in my heart you will always have a home

A fool for you

Complications of the heart cause us to not necessarily make the best decisions
We turn down a wrong road
Pick the wrong clothes
Say the wrong thing
And sometimes make the same mistakes

Over again
Apologizing for past sins
Forgiveness can't live
Where it can't get in

Saying I'm sorry
Making up with flowers and wanting
To just enjoy the peace of the moment
Of being with someone you love

Fighting and leaving
Fighting and needing you to just understand

Disappointments settling in
Here we go yet again
Trying to find our safe place
To let our feelings show
and cherish the love that we both know is there

Some say, "why stay?"
"Why go thru the pain?"
But I guess I'm just a fool for you.

Every time we go down that road
I think that I can't take it anymore
But I realize that love runs deep

It takes time to grow

Even more time to show
How good life will be
When twenty years down the road
Our story can be told
That love does conquer all

But until then
I will just be a fool for you.

come down

it's raining outside
and that's when i think of you
because you like the rain, the grey, the sound of the water on the ground

it comes down softly
in steady drops that wet everything around

i hear a melody in it
i see your face in the reflection of the water

i think of you
as the water falls down
making musical rhythms

letting me remember you.

swimming close to the edge

I'm trying to give it my all
I'm trying to give you my all

I breathe out slowly
lungs releasing heavy heated air into the outside

the restless nights have a familiar name, yours
written all over them

don't give up I say
your journey is still being traveled

I act strong to forget
but as soon as your gone I fall
again.

tantalized by your eyes
praying for moments of your passion
your space shared in mine
liking what you like
learning from your fingers
that continually play me

I say not again
but here you are
taking me too close to the edge

waiting, part two

I'm waiting for a love that will last
one that will not be in a rush to leave
one that won't make false promises
or hand me broken dreams

one that will hear me out
and forgive me of wrongs
or judge me and
one that sees the good
knowing that we belong

I'm waiting for a love to grow old with
who will hold my hand when i am cold
who will tell me they love me, even when I am stubborn

I'm waiting for a love that will light me from within
filling my heart with laughter and adventure still

I'm waiting for a true love
that doesn't play games

or force his way in

one that will unfold like a rose budding in spring
who rejoices in each other when discovering new things

I'm waiting for love

one that will hold true

comforting the hurt parts
making them new

I'm waiting for your love

the call

i pick up the phone
looking at it several times
picturing your name across the message line

i pick up my phone
thought it would ring
feeling it vibrate
with your number on the screen

i pick up the phone dialing
you again
getting to the last digit
but stopping before send

i remember all the words
i remember all the pain
how you were angry at me
how you left my hands again

it seems that we have said it once
said it all before
so i place my phone back upon the floor

i pick up my phone
looking at it still

thinking "today he'll call"
today he will

i think of you
not knowing if you are thinking of me

i'm losing sleep
losing hope
losing me

i can't seem to stop crying
i can't seem to make it right
i can't call you anymore
because i don't want to fight

i pushed you away
when i wanted you near
hoping you would understand
that i was living in fear

being alone was something that i was accustomed to
thinking everyone i loved would leave me
so i tested this theory and you made it true

when perfection wasn't enough
you were through

making bad choices
i pushed you farther away

hoping you would tenderly love
all the fear away

i pick up the phone
just to check it before i sleep

maybe he called
i just didn't hear it, maybe

feels like home

nothing compares to the awakening inside when they feel like home
the time seems longer and the days seem filled with moments you have yet to share
but it feels right, like home

warm apple pie on thanksgiving day
is what i remember when holding you in my arms

your kisses feel like rain in the summer time
on the Texas plains.

your voice takes me to a quiet time
watching the sun go down

and you remind me of home.

Your face is a present on Christmas day
and your laughter like a candy apple at the state fair.

your voice like a good movie with buttered popcorn and raisinettes

you remind me of home,

of good times,
of comfort and acceptance,
of lifelong episodes of love, family, and learning

you bring me home.

Suddenly

Suddenly you awake after being in a daze for so long
Transfixed on a certain spot perplexed by life's ever winding roads and mishaps

And then light
Approaching from the corners cascading into your heart
Quickens you, opening wondrous windows of possibilities

Dispelling the old ways of thinking and responding
Bringing renewed admiration and dedication for the things that matter most

Suddenly you have entered my life
You have made your mark
Just when I was giving up
There you were
Suddenly

something new

I'm finding myself wanting to be near you more
pondering how you are and who you are

By surprise you have occupied space
left abandoned by fate
receptive not at first, because damage had been done

then you smiled
shy at our first meeting
unable to look at me

I knew not what to expect but I would take a chance
I desired the chance
for something new.

moving like a car picking up speed
I'm falling hard, and fast

with nervous trepidation
I will only ask for more of you,

soliciting your timid glances and
your strong embraces

loving you in the day
kissing you in the night

what manifestation is this
of a chance meeting on a not so special eve

too soon to describe
though not too soon to feel

wishing on stars
never took me far, but when i wake in the morning

I realize that everything is good
because of you
my something new.

you

thinking of you
daydreaming
 mind wondering, time passing by slowly

still, frozen in space
the world moving around me feverishly

buzzing, humming,
people about their day,

sun shine, down time, i'm thinking of you.

i tell myself to relax and it will be fine
that school crushes do go the mile

it's okay to fall into love
and it just takes time.

i see your face, i feel your embrace
holding onto that image as i am drawn into a gaze

a small spot on the wall
and it doesn't move
i don't blink
i sit there
i try to focus
but its clearly hopeless
because i am thinking of you.

secret place

every discerning word inside

words you live by, words to hide

things one tries not to display, are often noticed

by careful eyes,

eyes that see way past the disguise.

lips conceal what truly only the heart can know

but limbs portray a foretold show

where the story begins with an innocent stare

pretending that no one was there

your secret place is where you reside.

your place to hide

the things you don't say

but do, only after making one believe in you

your secret place where memories live on

replaced by another face yet still singing the same song

detrimental to what could be

I sift through the stories, the places, and other things

looking for you

there in your secret place.

Falling in love

surreal

who can measure what
this thing called love is

initial attraction

I like the way you look
you smell good
your eyes are pretty

caught

I can't get you out of my mind
every song is on rewind
every movie i see is about love
everything reminds me of you
can i call you?
can i see you?

depth

I want to know you
where did you come from?
how can this be
we have so much in common
or do we
what's your family like?
god i want to hear you laugh
can you spend the night?

  time

My morning starts with you upon the rays of the sun cresting the eastern horizon
I look over with grateful heart that you are here with me
that in the midst of chaos we found each other
we talk
we disagree
we mingle, we stroll
we chat, we resign
we
just you and me

acceptance

I will not change you
respect makes us grow
to hold each other with esteem
and lift our souls
no harm will come to you
because of love
it changed me, you have changed me

change of heart

you found me in a broken place
exhausted from what was

disillusioned by promises
that never came to be

you appeared and helped me
 believe again.

I thought I knew what I wanted
I thought I would not heal
I thought that you only get a few tries
to make your mark at love and seal the deal

If that stood true
I was way past my limit
and for sure to be bitter after the emotional storm finished

but your ease of being
and kisses in morning

has introduced me to a new song.

although it didn't seem I was ready
and it may have been quick at the start,

but falling for you
has comforted me so
and given me a change of heart

I count the moments we spend together as life lessons coming to pass
learning from you, enjoying your company, and waiting to make you
smile.

I want to leave my mark
on your heart
just as you have left yours unexpectedly on mine.

Beauty in Ashes

Your home is burning Engulfed in flames
You are standing watching.
Everything you have is in that home,
All your possessions, memories and hopes
Unable to act or respond
The fire consumes all that you are

Eyes red. Choking on fumes, retracting from the heat
Helplessly you stand Not knowing what tomorrow will bring
It had not occurred to you in that moment
there was life after this
Nor would there be a home

All you see is now
The flames, the crumbling structure,
the roar of the beast that has your life in its grasp
 But after the fire has burned out
The noise has stopped
The ashes settle

Smokey snowflakes resting upon your head
You remember, your loved ones are safe
You are safe

You think of what was really in the house..
pictures, clothes, dishes Stuff. Material things

The truth is you needed a new kitchen
You wanted hardwood floors
Your plumbing was bad
 You didn't think of this as the disaster was happening,
for all we can see is the pain of now

There is truth in the ashes. There is beauty in the ashes

The fire took your old home
and what you thought was your life
Only to allow for you to have
what you truly want and cherish
those things that really matter.

There is beauty in the fire
And beauty in the ashes

Depths Below

to the bowels are they given
deep desires
saturated in deceit and contention

 the ugliness of distrust and manipulation

the border of sanity
bleakly remains in view
fading ever so swiftly
after every unforeseen incident

the gnawing away of one's soul
slowly depriving the human psyche of what it needs
 denying comfort
that would yet quench enough to persist

seeing those for who they really are
extinguishes the light inside
examining the right from wrong
we hope for clarity in darkness
and wish for the good in man

yet bitterness remains
day, after day and then night

no peace, no salvation

in this state we remain
until that self inside oneself
is at one with what is

the acceptance of the present
the wholehearted embrace of that which is tormented
can be forgiven

and then spring forth into a new self
as enlightened through the darkness
to once and for all reveal the true nature

as the cycle of life, death , and rebirth persist
and continues

to truly know
thyself is to delve into the depths below
those hidden parts, to make peace with them
and like a butterfly from a cocoon
take flight from the sluggish past of our old journey
to soar into the new.

Picture Perfect

often I think of what life could bring to me
of what shape and size
what time will the thing i need come to be

often i wait
impatiently, riddled with anxiety
focused too hard, too long on things that shouldn't matter it seems.

tired nights spent
wishing you were here
praying, and hoping in my unspoken mind
that you would appear.

analyzing to death all the possible outcomes
gearing myself for whatever the final decision was,

when will my story change, prosperity lean my way
to lay down the heaviness of this day
to not feel the need to be the master nor the slave

often I contemplate, at which day will my heart be at ease
the day that I can relax, and be free to just be.

the days do tread on,
and my soul and spirit are somewhat worn
although the fight in me still strives at its on will

I think I must give it all, to him I must give.

To many days have gone by
to not value what I have found,
admiration, passion, comfort, and I desire to know you more in and out.

I wondered why life had seemingly been cruel,

why when love is found it is just as quickly lost or misused,

why we gamble with our lies
why insecurity has us bound, to a life that wants us not, yet tarry we do

I wondered about life considering me and you,
if I want you too much, or is the moment sincere
laying in your arms saying sweet adieu

often i questioned
until the morning came, you were still there, just the same
time replaced my doubt,
your eyes erased my fear
the picture of us displayed for all to see
made everything clear.

I love you

I pour out

I pour out my heart to thee overflowing
and full of compassion

let it cover you
let it carry you through

as breath remains
let my love drench your soul and spirit

reaching out my hand to comfort you
know that it is I that cares
and who sees the best in you

I pour out my song to thee
of your kindness, of your mercy, and your patience

Favor finds me as I bow out
when I no longer can stand
I yield to you
the great unknown who holds the world forever in his hands

capturing me so that i in turn
can hold you
grant me the peace in all things
so that my portion to lend will be the same

I pour out all of me
exposed for the world to see
faults, flaws and all

take me as I am
no angel, not a saint, nor a sinner

a man, just a man.

You were made for me

you were made for me
time between us doesn't fade the desire i feel for you
the hours of the day pass with ease
but you remain in them, every second of every minute
thinking of you

where are you
what are you doing
who are you with

i know the answers to these questions
or at least i think
i ache
i quake inside for you

i hid from you
i escaped from you
pushing you farther away

wanting you more
wanting you near
but at a distance

please don't push don't barge
just ask
that i may let you into my heart

fragile i am
broken i am

made for me you are
roses and cards
hugs and kisses
simple for sane
the ordinary love explained

i needed just an acknowledgement of love
that i exist
that i matter

and there you were
found
not in a search,
but presented
as a gift
an answer to a prayer
that says you are enough

you were made for me

in my mind

to love, to lose
to have, to hold
the picture reminiscent of what was once us

illusion or not
to will, to want
is this real?

I ponder and mull it over in my mind
contemplating a leap of faith
but will it be worth it?
or am I just deluding myself with false fantasies.

you are so that I am alone but seeing the future
while in my sleep I rise with a sense of calm
believing wholeheartedly that we will be
not too often do I linger in dreams
but all too real
it seems to be my destiny

sensing some finalization
yet I remain adamant about my affection
hoping to find truth at the heart of the matter
letting all the pieces fall into place
one at a time
slowly realizing the picture looks better when complete

am I dreaming?
when will i awake?

It won't always be like this

"it won't always be like this" the little voice says
you always get what you need
you are always in good care.

you won't have to wonder
too much more
because the thing you need is at your door

"it won't always be like this" the voice says again
when that time comes
you will feel it from within.

You will know when to let go
the right thing to say
you may not have to raise a finger
or have some over-the-top display

it will come with ease
and it will be alright
it will be perfectly clear,
like a hanging star on a moonless mountaintop night.

better days will come
as time progresses at its on pace
there's no need to rush,
just be patient
just wait

enjoy the moment,
let the peace flow
bask in each syllable, each pixilated image
tone, color, temperature, and scent

and then you will
find your moment,

to rise above and know that it is time
to accept a better world for life, for mine

to walk into your destiny of a finer self
releasing the things that held you back
their ungrateful overlooking all the precious things you have

endure just a little bit more
it won't be like this always, of that I am sure.

Two hearts

One boy
One night
One change
One thought
One look
One smile
One touch
One kiss

Two dates

One beach
One trip

Three dates

One feeling; love
One hope; trust

Two hearts started as strangers
Ending as lovers
Lasting as friends

Two hearts now one
Never alone
Never lost

pitfall

I have felt the depths of your love
Its very essence palpable

Tremors and tingles come in waves
From being next to you
Crashing into my soul
Washing over me

I gasp for air
Drowning in you

Don't throw out the line
I need not to be saved

Don't rescue me.

Let me sink slowly
Watching the last trace of light dissipate
Releasing my lungs of the fearful air
To be filled up by the heave fluid

Anticipation leading me further
Into unknown leagues

I smile knowing I will not return
To the place I once was before

I will never be the same
This watery grave is now my home

Buried in the sea of your love.

God smiles

On the next day it rises
With the eastern sun

Then it sits on clouds
Until the day is done

It nourished the plants and trees to grow
It comes and melts the frigid ice and cold

It makes us happy to be alive
It firms our soggy foundation
Making it solid ground

It reminds us to be thankful
After the rain has come

To also be thankful for the shade of the trees
And a roof of a home

When he smiles things must change
Where the sun remains

Pillow talk

You tell me everything I want to hear

Whispering every word so sweet and so dear

While strumming my arm and grasping my hand

Priceless moments like these

Stolen by the moonlight

Just before the kiss goodnight

I believe what you say

Without question or charge

As we lay here

Still in bed

Enraptured in pillow talk

lost

I found love
Or so it seemed
How could it have taken so long to elude me?
From late night phone calls
To random people on the streets
Every place has been explored

With not one accomplished feat
I found love many times before.
Brilliant, aggressive, jealous and a bore
Tall, small, thick and thin
All vying for attention just to get in

Ups and downs, fights and wins
Make-up and break-ups
Sometimes on a coaster ride that won't end.
I found love or at least I thought

Until I was left speechless from just one

One look at you

Who took me by surprise

When I had given love its last try

Finally when I had stopped to enjoy

No regards, no present or awards

Love found me.

*"happiness is contagious,
if you don't catch it you might be immune"*

Dmarkis Wigfall

Dear Friends,

Thank you for taking this journey with me. Over 15 years of my life are in these pages. It is awesome to look back and remember each chapter that led to yet another life lesson. These moments that defined who I am today are easier to read than be done, especially when you are in the thick of it.

With each new story or poem I have grown so much and learned that if we never stop moving forward or bettering our internal selves we can experience every aspect of love even in its unexpected measures.

My last thoughts I would like to impart are to love hard, love indiscriminately, and love now. Every gift of charity that you give will return to you.

Dmarkis